BRITANNICA BEGINNER BIOS

STEVE JOBS
VISIONARY OF THE DIGITAL REVOLUTION

CHRISTINE HONDERS

Britannica®
Educational Publishing

IN ASSOCIATION WITH

ROSEN
EDUCATIONAL SERVICES

Published in 2016 by Britannica Educational Publishing (a trademark of Encyclopædia Britannica, Inc.) in association with The Rosen Publishing Group, Inc.
29 East 21st Street, New York, NY 10010

Distributed exclusively by Rosen Publishing.
To see additional Britannica Educational Publishing titles, go to rosenpublishing.com.

First Edition

Britannica Educational Publishing
J. E. Luebering: Director, Core Reference Group
Mary Rose McCudden: Editor, Britannica Student Encyclopedia

Rosen Publishing
Hope Lourie Killcoyne: Executive Editor
Heather Moore Niver: Editor
Nelson Sá: Art Director
Michael Moy: Designer
Cindy Reiman: Photography Manager

Library of Congress Cataloging-in-Publication Data

Honders, Christine, author.
Steve Jobs: Visionary of the Digital Revolution/Christine Honders.
     pages cm.—(Britannica beginner bios)
Includes bibliographical references and index.
ISBN 978-1-62275-921-7 (library bound)—ISBN 978-1-62275-923-1 (pbk.)—ISBN 978-1-62275-925-5 (6-pack)
1. Jobs, Steve, 1955-2011—Juvenile literature. 2. Computer engineers—United States—Biography—Juvenile literature. 3. Businesspeople—United States—Biography—Juvenile literature. 4. Computer industry—United States—Biography—Juvenile literature. 5. Apple Computer, Inc.—History—Juvenile literature. I. Title.
QA76.2.J63H66 2016
338.7'61004092—dc23
[B]
     2014039764

Manufactured in the United States of America

Photo credits: Cover, pp. 4, 16, 27 Justin Sullivan/Getty Images; p. 1, interior pages (background) John Lamb/Photodisc/Getty Images; p. 5 Glen Wilson/©Open Road Films/courtesy Everett Collection; p. 6 optimarc/Shutterstock.com; p. 7 Photoshot/Everett Collection; p. 8 turtix/Shutterstock.com; pp. 9, 11 (bottom), 17 Ted Thai/The Life Picture Collection/Getty Images; p. 10 TonyV3112/Shutterstock.com; p. 11 (top) Science & Society Picture Library/Getty Images; p. 12 © AP Images; p. 13 Michael L Abramson/Archive Photos/Getty Images; p. 15 © Walt Disney Pictures/Entertainment Pictures/ZUMA Press; pp. 18, 25 Bloomberg/Getty Images; p. 21 Maridav/Shutterstock.com; p. 22 Sathit/Shutterstock.com; p. 24 Ulrich Baumgarten/Getty Images.

CONTENTS

CHAPTER ONE

FOUNDER OF APPLE

It's hard to imagine a world without computers. They're in our homes, in cars, and in stores. Some people carry computers everywhere they go! It hasn't always been that way. The first computers were made more than 70 years ago, but they were very big and complicated. In 1975, the first home computer was created. A year later, a young man and his friend showed the world their invention, a computer called the Apple I. The man's name was Steve Jobs.

In 1976, Steve Jobs created Apple, which was one of the first companies that made computers that people could use at home.

Steve Jobs and his friend Stephen Wozniak founded a company called Apple as well. Apple is now one of the most successful companies in the world. As the head of Apple, Steve Jobs helped invent the first Apple computer, the Macintosh computer, and the iPhone, just to name a few. His inventions changed the way people learn about things and how they **COMMUNICATE** with each other.

It wasn't easy for Steve Jobs to become one of the most important inventors of our time. His success was the result of a lot of hard work. He was always thinking of ways to make his inventions better and better.

In 2013 a movie was made about Jobs. It showed how hard he worked on all of the products he created.

CHAPTER TWO

EARLY LIFE

Jobs was born on February 24, 1955, in San Francisco, California. He was adopted by Clara and Paul Jobs, who gave him the name Steven Paul. He had a younger sister named Patricia. The family moved to Mountain View, California, when Steve was five.

When he was a kid, he liked reading, swimming, music, and playing jokes on people. Sometimes, he fooled around in class so much that he drove his teachers crazy! Even though he didn't always do well in school, he was smart. His father showed him how to take apart radios and televisions and put them back

Jobs's father taught him how to take apart electronics and put them back together. This showed him the importance of knowing how things work, inside and out.

The first project Jobs (*left*) and Wozniak (*right*) ever made together was called a blue box. It let them make free phone calls.

together. This hobby helped him learn a lot about electronics.

As a teenager, Jobs got a summer job at an electronics company. In high school, he joined an electronics club whose members were called "wireheads." He also met Stephen Wozniak, or "Woz," as everyone called him. Jobs didn't know it at the time, but Wozniak would one day be his business partner. Back then they were just good friends who loved electronics.

In 1972, Jobs went to Reed College. He left school after less than a year but stayed in the area and took a few classes. In 1974, he briefly worked at Atari, a video-game company. Later that year he traveled to India and then returned to California. He met his old friend Wozniak, and together they built a computer...right in Jobs's garage!

Jobs wanted to build more computers so that they could sell them. They didn't have enough money, so Jobs sold his car and Wozniak sold his prized scientific calculator. After that, their company, named Apple, was born. Wozniak did the building, and Jobs designed the computers. They made a great team.

Jobs and Wozniak built their first computer in the garage of the California home where Jobs grew up.

Jobs is shown here with the Apple II. It was the first computer that could play sounds and show pictures in color.

People liked the Apple I computers, but Jobs and Wozniak wanted to make them even better. In 1977, the Apple II was created. It was smaller, faster, and easier for people to use. Many people say that the Apple II started the home computer revolution. Apple became one of the biggest companies in the United States.

Quick Fact

Jobs and Wozniak couldn't come up with a good name for their new company. One day, after Jobs returned from a trip to an apple orchard, he suggested the name "Apple." They tried to come up with a more technical name but couldn't, so the name "Apple" stuck.

9

CHAPTER THREE

RISE AND FALL WITH APPLE

Apple II computers were sold all over the world, and Apple made millions of dollars. However, the next two computers that Apple made didn't work as well as the Apple II. So people didn't want to buy them.

Another problem was that another company, IBM, started making home computers, too. Apple was a brand-new company. IBM was already well known, and people bought more computers from it. Jobs started working on

An apple has been the symbol for the company Apple since it started in 1976.

This IBM XT computer, which was made in 1983, had more memory than any other home computer.

new computers that he hoped would change that situation.

In 1983, Apple released the Lisa computer. The following year the company introduced the Macintosh, or Mac. They were the first computers to feature a mouse and a picture-based screen. This means that a person could move a pointer on the screen and click on pictures that would tell the computer what to do. Today that is common, but at the time it was a major invention.

Steve Jobs sits with the Lisa computer, which he named after his daughter.

However, the computers didn't sell as well as Jobs thought they would. The Lisa was too expensive and not very powerful. The Macintosh could not run the **SOFTWARE** that the IBM computers used. People wanted to be able to use the same programs on any computer. So, even though the Macintosh was easier to use and had new and improved technology, it was not popular with many people at first.

Vocabulary
SOFTWARE is programs and instructions that tell a computer what to do.

The Macintosh featured a revolutionary picture-based screen and a mouse. But customers were reluctant to buy the expensive computer, in part because it used special software.

12

When Macintosh computers failed to sell as well as Apple hoped, the company leaders blamed Jobs. In 1985, Jobs left the company.

By this time, Apple was a huge company that was run by people other than Jobs. The people in charge of Apple blamed Jobs for the poor sales of the Macintosh and wanted him to leave. He quit in 1985.

Quick Fact
Steve Jobs didn't always want to be an inventor. When he was a teen he became interested in the religion of Buddhism. He even went to India to study Buddhism.

CHAPTER FOUR

FROM PIXAR, BACK TO APPLE

Some people would give up after so many failures. But not Steve Jobs! He never gave up on his dreams of making technology better and better.

Jobs believed he could create better computers than the ones people were using. He started a new computer company called NeXT. Then, in 1986 he decided to buy a company from director, writer, and producer George Lucas. The company used computer technology to create graphics, or illustrations, for films. It became known as Pixar. In 1991, Pixar made a deal with Disney to make a computer-animated movie. Four years later, the movie *Toy Story* was released, and it was a huge hit! After *Toy Story*, Pixar

In 1995, *Toy Story* made more money than any other film. It made $192 million in the United States and $362 million around the world.

Animation Studios produced many more popular films, including *A Bug's Life, Finding Nemo,* and *The Incredibles.*

Meanwhile, by the mid-1990s, Apple was failing. Another computer company named Microsoft was much more popular than Apple. Jobs's computer company NeXT had created an **OPERATING SYSTEM** called NeXTSTEP. NeXTSTEP could compete with Windows, which was the system Microsoft used. Apple wanted to buy NeXTSTEP, and Jobs convinced

When Jobs took over Pixar, there were only 44 employees. Today, more than 1,000 people work at Pixar, which has made dozens of films.

When he returned to work at Apple, Jobs designed computers such as the iBook, shown here, the brightly colored, portable version of an iMac.

Vocabulary

The **OPERATING SYSTEM** is the main software in a computer that controls how it works.

it to buy the whole company! Twelve years after he left Apple, Steve Jobs was back in charge of the company he started.

Jobs began designing new computers that would save his company. The first computer to come out after his return to Apple was the iMac. The iMac was different from any other computer because it came in lots of

17

bright colors. Jobs said, "The back of our computer looks better than the front of their computers."

But looks weren't the only thing that made iMacs better. Jobs, as always, wanted to make sure that they were good computers that were also easy for people to use. The iMac system was an integrated

The first iPhone was released in 2007. Within three months one million were sold.

Quick Fact

Jobs's father taught him that the back of a chest of drawers should be as beautiful as the front because the quality should be the same throughout.

system, which meant that the hardware and software all came together with the computer. This made it very easy to use. Other computers had lots of different parts made by different companies, which could be confusing.

Steve Jobs's creativity didn't stop at computers. Around 1998, MP3 players were becoming popular. These are small devices that store and play music. Jobs did not like the players that were available. So he and his team invented a new MP3 player, and in 2001, the iPod was born. It was faster and stored much more music than other MP3 players. The iPod quickly became the best-selling MP3 player in the world.

> **Quick Fact**
> Apple has sold millions of its iPhones. In 2014, it sold 10 million iPhone 6 and 6 Plus units in just three days.

But he did not stop there. The success of the iPod made Jobs think that Apple could become the greatest electronics company in the world. Cell phones were becoming popular. Jobs wanted to make a cell phone that could make phone calls, play music, and let people use the Internet.

Jobs started to work on a phone that didn't have buttons. He and his team created what is called touch screen technology, meaning people could touch pictures, letters, and numbers on a screen and make the phone do what they wanted it to do. In 2007, Apple released the first iPhone. No one had ever seen anything like it before.

Touch screen technology was the wave of the future. Jobs knew that this technology wouldn't just

Tablets, such as the iPad, and smartphones are minicomputers that can be taken anywhere in the world!

be useful for phones. He also thought that people were ready for something even better than a computer. In 2010, the iPad was released as the first tablet computer. It was a computer, a gaming **DEVICE**, and a way to connect with people all over the world.

Vocabulary
A DEVICE is a piece of equipment that is made for a special purpose.

CHAPTER FIVE

VISIONARY

People wait at Apple stores for hours, even days, whenever Apple releases a new product.

By 2014, Apple said that it had sold more than 300 million iPods, more than 100 million iPhones, and more than 15 million iPads. Apple has also been listed as number one on *Fortune* magazine's list of "America's Most Admired Companies." Apple might not have been this successful if it wasn't for Steve Jobs.

So what made Jobs such a leader? He was very smart, but he didn't make his inventions by himself. Other people on his teams built the computers, phones, and tablets. What he did was make these inventions even better.

Jobs cared about the technology that went into his products, and he wanted to know every detail. He wanted the inside of his computers to look as good as the outside. He was like an artist: Jobs cared about what color each screw was even if you couldn't see it! Design was very important to him.

Quick Fact

Jobs's favorite clothes to wear were black turtlenecks and jeans. In fact, he owned more than 100 pairs of jeans!

Jobs cared about every detail in every invention, such as the motherboard inside this Apple Power Mac G4 computer.

Jobs was a perfectionist, and he spent hours testing and retesting all his new products. If he didn't like something, he would go back to his team and

Touch screen technology made Apple's iPods and iPhones easy for people to use.

tell them to make it again until he thought it was right. And he would do this over and over again! If he thought something was too complicated, he would tell his team to make it simpler. He thought the products should be easy for people to use. Jobs could be difficult to work for, but his workers were loyal to him. He was very good at getting them to do their best.

In 2003, Steve Jobs became sick. He had a tumor on his pancreas and needed to have an operation to remove it. It turned out that Jobs had cancer. But even being ill didn't stop him from running his company. He stayed on as the head of Apple until he became so sick that he couldn't work anymore. He gave up his job as head of Apple in August 2011. On October 5, 2011, Steve Jobs died.

Steve Jobs was more than an inventor. He was a VISIONARY. Even after some of his inventions didn't do

Vocabulary

A **VISIONARY** is someone who thinks about or plans the future with imagination and knowledge.

Steve Jobs once said, "Going to bed at night saying we've done something wonderful . . . that's what matters to me."

well, and even after he was forced to leave his company, he never gave up on his ideas. It was this way of thinking that made Apple one of the most successful companies of all time. And it was this way of thinking that made Steve Jobs one of the most successful company leaders and inventors of all time.

TIMELINE

1955: Steven Paul Jobs is born on February 24 and adopted by Clara and Paul Jobs.

1969: Jobs meets Stephen Wozniak.

1973: Jobs briefly attends Reed College.

1976: Jobs and Wozniak make the Apple I and form the Apple company.

1977: The Apple II is invented, and Apple becomes a big success.

1980: The Apple III is invented, but it is not popular.

1983: The Lisa computer is released. It also does not sell well.

1984: Apple releases the Macintosh.

1985: Jobs quits Apple and starts his own computer company, NeXT.

1986: Jobs buys Pixar.

1991: Pixar makes a deal with Disney to make a movie.

1992: NeXT makes an operating system called NeXTSTEP.

1995: Pixar releases the first computer animated movie, *Toy Story*.

1997: Jobs goes back to Apple and becomes the company leader.

1998: Apple releases the iMac computer.

2001: The first iPod is produced.

2003: The iTunes online music store opens.

2003: Jobs learns he has pancreatic cancer.

2005: The iPod Shuffle, a smaller version of the iPod, is released.

2007: Jobs introduces the iPhone and touch screen technology.

2009: Jobs takes six months off because of his bad health.

2010: The iPad is released.

2011: Jobs steps down as the leader of Apple in August.

2011: Steve Jobs dies on October 5.

GLOSSARY

ANIMATION The art and science of making pictures, or images, appear to move.

DESIGN To create for a specific function or end.

GRAPHICS Pictures, maps, or graphs used for illustration.

HARDWARE The physical components of a computer.

INTEGRATED Having different parts working together as one.

INVENTOR Someone who creates or produces something for the first time.

PANCREAS A gland inside the body near the stomach that helps the body digest food.

PERFECTIONIST Someone who wants everything to be just right.

REVOLUTION A sudden, extreme, or complete change.

STORE To place in a computer's memory.

TECHNOLOGY The use of science in solving problems.

BOOKS

Gould, Jane. *Steve Jobs*. New York, NY: PowerKids Press, 2013.

Lakin, Patricia. *Steve Jobs: Thinking Differently*. New York, NY: Aladdin, 2012.

Pollack, Pamela D., and Meg Belviso. *Who Was Steve Jobs?* New York, NY: Grosset and Dunlap, 2012.

Ziller, Amanda. *Steve Jobs: American Genius*. New York, New York: Harper-Collins, 2012.

WEBSITES

Because of the changing nature of Internet links, Rosen Publishing has developed an online list of websites related to the subject of this book. This site is updated regularly. Please use this link to access this list:

http://www.rosenlinks.com/BBB/Jobs

INDEX